A Kid's Guide to
AUSTRALIA

A koala taking a little snooze.

Jack L. Roberts

Curious Kids Press • Palm Springs, CA
www.curiouskidspress.com

Publisher: *Curious Kids Press, Palm Springs, CA 92264.*
Designed by: *Michael Owens*
Editor: *Sterling Moss*
Copy Editor: *Janice Ross*

Table of Contents

Uluru (aka Ayers Rock), located outside of Alice Springs in the Australian outback, is the largest rock in the world. It's 1,100 feet (335 meters) tall.

G'Day, Mate. Welcome to Australia.

THE FIRST THING MOST PEOPLE THINK ABOUT when it comes to Australia is the kangaroo. And for good reason. Australia and the neighboring island of Papua New Guinea are the only two countries in the world where these unique **mammals** live.

But there is much more to Australia than kangaroos -- from the Great Barrier Reef to the Aboriginal peoples to the wide open spaces of the Australian outback.

Read on to discover more about this awesome country. One thing is for sure. Wherever you go, you're sure to hear the friendly Aussie greeting -- "G'day, Mate.

Your Passport to Australia

The Australian Flag has a blue background with the Union Jack (the flag of the United Kingdom) in the upper left corner. It has a large white commonwealth star with seven points below the Union Jack. The right side has five stars that represent the Southern Cross constellation.

Official Name: Commonwealth of Australia
Capital City: Canberra
Country Area (Size): 2,988,901 sq. miles (7,741,220 sq. km); slightly smaller than the continental U.S.
Population: 22,751,014
Official Language: English
Currency: Australian dollar

PASSPORT

States
ica

WHere IN THe WorLd IS AustraLia?

YOU'VE PROBABLY HEARD PEOPLE SAY that Australia is a country "down under." But where exactly is "down under"? The term comes from the fact that Australia is located below the **equator**. It is in the Southern Hemisphere between the Pacific Ocean (to the east) and the Indian Ocean (to the west).

Australia shares no land borders with any other country. In fact, the closest country to Australia is 1,471 miles (2,368 km) away. That country is Papua New Guinea. Even New Zealand, which many people often think is close to Australia, is actually more than 2,581 miles (4,154 km) away. That's about as far as it is from Philadelphia to Los Angeles.

This awesome country is the sixth largest country (by area) in the world. It is also both the world's largest island and the world's smallest continent.

Did You Know? No part of Australia is more than 621 miles (1000 km) from the ocean and a beach.

The 6 States of Australia

AUSTRALIA IS DIVIDED into six states (Southern Australia, Western Australia, New South Wales, Queensland, Victoria, and Tasmania). It also consists of two major mainland territories—the Australia Capital Territory (ACT) and the Northern Territory (NT). Both territories function (or work) very much like states.

Five of Australia's six states are part of the mainland. The sixth state – Tasmania -- is an island 150 miles (240 km) to the south of the mainland.

A Brief History of Australia

60,000-40,000 B.C. People from Southeast Asia settle in Australia. (Their descendants are the Aboriginal people.)

1770: British explorer James Cook arrives in Australia. He claims it for Great Britain and names it New South Wales.

1778: 1,400 people (mostly convicts) arrive from England and establish the British Crown Colony of New South Wales.

1851: Gold is found in southern Australia creating a "gold rush," just like the Gold Rush in California in 1849. The discovery brings thousands of immigrants to Australia.

19th century: Six separate colonies are formed.

1901: The six colonies join to form the Commonwealth of Australia with a democratic government.

1927: Canberra becomes the nation's capital.

1956: Melbourne hosts the Olympic Games; Sydney hosts the 2000 Summer Games.

1962: Aborigines are given the right to vote; five years later, they become Australian citizens.

2008: The Australian parliament formally apologizes for past wrongs committed against the Aboriginal people

Photo: *Aboriginal rock art in Western Australia.*

Cool Facts About Australia

The Aborigines invented the boomerang around 8,000 B.C. When this wooden weapon is thrown, it returns to its thrower.

The Sydney funnel-web spider is considered to be the world's most-deadly spider.

It can kill you in less than two hours.

In 1902, Australia became the second country in the world to give women the right to vote. (New Zealand was first in 1893).

The Sydney Opera House is one of the most amazing structures ever designed. Look at the roof. What does it look like to you? The architect says he got his idea for the design from the way an orange breaks apart.

It may come as a surprise to learn that the Australian Alps receive more snow each year than Switzerland!

Fun Things For Kids to Do in the Land Down Under

NO MATTER WHERE YOU GO in Australia, there is always something fun, interesting, and exciting to do. Here are just a few of the things to do in the land down under.

1. Climb to the top of The Sydney Harbour Bridge.

Climb to the top of the Sydney Harbour Bridge (aka the "coat hanger" bridge because of its arch-based construction). You'll get a spectacular view of all of Sydney – 440 ft. (134 m) above sea level!

2. Go Gold Prospecting in Western Australia.

Try your luck at gold prospecting in the heart of Western Australia's Golden Outback, the area that thousands of fortune-seekers rushed to after the discovery of gold in the 1880's.

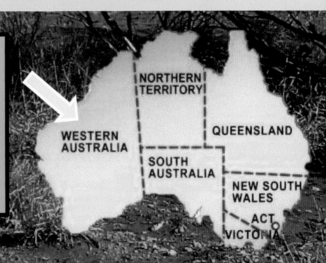

3. Visit the Towering Twelve Apostles.

Take a drive along Great Ocean Road which winds for 150 miles (243 km) along the Southern Ocean. Be sure to check out **The Towering Twelve Apostles**, an amazing collection of rock formations.

4. Take A 6-day bushwalk

Take a 6-day, 40 mile (65km) bushwalk on the *Overland Track*, one of Australia's most famous hiking trails. It's located in the Cradle Mountain-Lake St. Clair National Park, on the island of Tasmania.

5. Visit the Great Barrier Reef.

THE SPRAWLING GREAT BARRIER REEF is the world's largest coral reef system. It is also the largest structure on Earth made by living organisms and the only living thing on Earth that astronauts can see from space.

The Great Barrier Reef is one of the Seven Wonders of the Natural World. It ranks right up there with Mount Everest and The Grand Canyon (two other "wonders of the natural world.")

The Great Barrier Reef consists of 2,900 individual reefs off the coast of Queensland in northeast Australia. It stretches more than 1,400 miles (2,300 kilometers) – about the distance from Boston to Miami. It also covers an area of 133,000 square miles 344,468 sq. km).

6. Go Snorkeling over Great Barrier Reef.

Go snorkeling* over The Great Barrier Reef, an underwater ecosystem often called the "rainforest of the sea." It's about the size of Texas. That's pretty amazing!

*Be careful: When snorkeling on or near coral reefs, avoid coming in contact with the delicate (and sometimes sharp) coral.

FUN Things For Kids to Do, cont.

7. Visit the Animals on Kangaroo Island

WITH A NAME LIKE KANGAROO ISLAND, it's got to be fun, right? And it is. You can see seals, dolphins, and wallabies. You can also see echidnas. (That's a type of anteater.) Oh, yeah, there are also plenty of kangaroos. They are the smallest of all kangaroos. They are known as Kangaroo Island kangaroos.

On Kangaroo Island (called just KI), kids can hand-feed kangaroos, koalas, and other animals. More than 1,500 different kinds of animals live on Kangaroo Island.

How to Speak Aussie

AUSTRALIAN PEOPLE (or "Aussies" as they are sometimes called) have a funny way of talking. At least, it sounds funny to some American ears. But you can start to learn to speak like an Aussie by picking up just a few special words. Here are some of them. In no time, you'll be talking like a "dinky-di Aussie – that's a born and bred Australian.

candy — lollies

Barbeque or cookout — barbie

pants — daks

COOKIE — BISCUIT

flashlight — torch

good bye — hooroo

diaper — nappy

bathroom — dunnie

The Kangaroo
and Other Australian Animals

Hi, Guys.

THE KANGAROO IS A MARSUPIAL. A marsupial carries its newborn in a pouch. Other well-known marsupials include the koala, the wombat, and the scary Tasmania devil. (See page 20.) Most marsupials live in Australia. The only marsupial that lives in the U.S. is the opossum.

The Red Kangaroo

MANY PEOPLE THINK that all kangaroos are the same. Not true. In fact, there are six different species (or kinds) of kangaroos in Australia. The largest is the Red Kangaroo. (It's also the largest marsupial on Earth.)

Kangaroos are unique in one other way. They are the only large mammals that hop as a means of getting around. Most kangaroos can hop at speeds up to 40 mph (60 km/h). They use their thick long tail to balance them while hopping.

THE KOALA

IT'S A CUTE, CUDDLY ANIMAL. Many people call it the koala *bear*. But it's not a bear at all. It's a marsupial, just like the kangaroo. It loves to eat the leaves of eucalyptus trees. But many of those trees are being cut down. So the koala is losing its natural **habitat**. When a koala is born, it is about as big as a jellybean. Imagine! It lives in its mother's pouch for the first five or six months.

THE PLATYPUS

THE PLATYPUS is a funny animal. (Just the sound of its name is funny.) It looks like three different animals. It has a paddle-shaped tail. That is like a beaver. It has a furry body. That is like an otter. It also has a flat bill and webbed feet. Yup, just like a duck. Weird, huh? It also doesn't have teeth! The platypus lives only in certain parts of Australia and Tasmania.

Did You Know?

The male platypus is **venomous**. It has sharp stingers on the rear of its feet. The stingers can send out a strong poison if the platypus feels threatened. The poison is not strong enough to kill a human, but it can sure hurt for a long time.

The Tasmanian Devil

THE TASMANIAN DEVIL is a scary-looking little, uh, creature, isn't he? He's found in the wild only in Tasmania. No surprise there, given the name. It's a **carnivorous** marsupial and the size of a small dog. People who know say that these little devils are not dangerous – at least to people. But we don't think they'll make a good family pet any time soon.

The Tree Kangaroo

TAKE A LOOK AT the cute little guy in the picture. It looks like a cross between a kangaroo and a lemur, don't you think? Actually, it is a **tree-kangaroo.**

The tree-kangaroo lives mostly in the upper branches of trees of the tropical rain forests of Papua New Guinea and parts of Queensland, Australia.

Today, tree-kangaroos are in danger of extinction. They are losing their habitat due to **deforestation** and poaching (the illegal hunting or trapping of animals).

THe DiNGo

THE DINGO IS A WILD DOG found only in Australia and Southeast Asia.

Some experts say that a dingo can make a great pet. It just needs to be trained as a pet almost from the time it is born.

Dingoes have unique wrists – almost like a human wrist. They can use their paws to turn a door knob. The dingo can also turn its head almost half-way around in either direction.

Did You Know?

Unlike dogs, dingoes do not bark. They howl – like wolves.

The Australian Outback

MORE THAN 50,000 YEARS AGO, a group of people traveled from Asia across **land bridges** to a new home. They settled in the center of present-day Australia. It was a remote and harsh area and a difficult place to live.

Today, descendants of those early travelers live throughout Australia. They live in cities and towns. Some are doctors and teachers; others are writers and political leaders. They are known as the Aboriginal people or the Aborigines.

But many Aboriginal people also still live in what is known as the Australian outback. That word refers to the vast interior regions of Australia. The word got started in the late 1800s, as Australia was being colonized. People would often talk about the settlements in the center of this huge country. When they did, they would often say, "out in the back settlements." Bingo. The word "outback" was born.

Photo: Rock paintings In Western Australia

Alice Springs

ONE OF THE MOST WELL-KNOWN TOWNS IN THE AUSTRALIAN OUTBACK is Alice Springs. It is roughly in the center of the outback (which itself is in the center of the Australian continent). Nearly 20 percent of the people in Alice Springs are Aboriginal Australians.

The town is famous as the Aboriginal Art capital of Central Australia. There are many Aboriginal art galleries in Alice Springs.

Alice Springs is more than 900 miles (1,500 km) from the nearest major city. Yet, it attracts tourists from around the world. They come to visit the Aboriginal people, but also to see the awesome desert landscape.

The Story of the Aboriginal People

Australian Aboriginal dancers.

TRIBES OF indigenous people (or Aborigines) have lived in Australia for thousands of years. Yet, when the British first arrived in Australia in 1788, they decided that no one "owned" the land. So they claimed the land for the king, as they began to colonize the country.

In 1901, Australia was declared an independent country. Aboriginal people, however, were not allowed to become citizens of the new country. That was bad enough. Yet, there was something even worse that went on.

Between 1910 and 1970, babies and children of Aboriginal parents were often taken from their families. The British believed that it was in the best interest of the child to be raised in a Christian family. The children were made to adopt the white culture. They were forbidden to speak their traditional language. Years later, these children became known as the Stolen Generations.

Finally, in 1967, the Aboriginal people were granted citizenship. But it took until 2008 for the Australian government to formally apologize to the Aborigines for the Stolen Generations. The government also apologized for other government laws that caused the Aboriginal population to suffer a great deal.

The didgeridoo (aka didjeridu) is an unusual musical instrument. It is a long hollow piece of wood. Some researchers believe it is the world's oldest musical instrument.

Think About This

What does a didgeridoo sound like? Some say it is very soothing and peaceful. One person said, "It sounds as if I'm flying over clouds." Awesome.

The Story of the Aboriginal People, CONT.

Traditional Aboriginal people believe that shared experiences are important. Whenever they meet someone new, they try to find something that they both have in common. Maybe it's someone they both know. Or maybe it's a place they've both been. A shared experience lays the groundwork for a good relationship.

An Aboriginal warrior shows a young girl how to throw a boomerang during a cultural show in Queensland.

Did You Know? The Australian Aboriginal culture is said to be the oldest continuous living culture on the planet.

The Torres Strait Islanders

The Torres Strait Islands are part of the Australian state of Queensland. The islands lie between Australia and Papua New Guinea. The first people came to the islands more than 70,000 years ago. Today, the descendants of those people are known as Torres Strait Islanders. They are Australia citizens.

Photo by Ludo Kuipers, 8/23/88

Dancers from the Torres Strait Islands perform a traditional dance.

THE TORRES STRAIT ISLANDER FLAG is very symbolic. The green horizontal panels at the top and the bottom of the flag symbolize the land. The blue panel in the center represents the waters of the Torres Strait. The thin black stipes represent the Torres Strait people. The white five-pointed star at the center of the flag represents the five major island groups. Finally, the white *dhari* (dancer's headdress) around the star also symbolize the Torres Strait Islands people.

The First European Settlers in Australia

The first Europeans arrived in Australia in 1788. They were mostly convicts. The British government sent them to this distant land as punishment for their crimes. Often, the crimes were minor, like stealing a loaf of bread. More convicts arrived over the next 80 years. Eventually, these convicts and their **descendants** built a great country.

Eleven ships from England arrived in Australia in 1788, carrying mostly convicts.

THINK OF THIS: In 1788, the trip from Europe to Australia by sea took 8 months. Today, the same trip by air takes 22 hours.

Just For Fun
Kangaroo Quiz: True or False

How much do you know about kangaroos? Let's find out. Read each statement below. Decide if it is true or false. Then check your answers on page 30..

1. If a kangaroo thinks there is danger in the area, it will stomp its foot on the ground to alert others.

2. Kangaroos are carnivores. They eat only meat.

3. Kangaroos are social and live in groups. Each group is called a mob.

4. When a joey is born, it can be as small as a grain of rice or as big as a bee (in other words, still pretty small).

5. Kangaroos can walk backwards.

Glossary

Aboriginal: Relating to the people who have been in a certain region from the earliest time.

Aborigine: A member of the original people in an area.

Bushwalk: A term used in Australia for both on- and off-trail hiking.

Carnivorous: Eating the flesh of animals.

Culture: The language, ideas, customs, beliefs, and art of a particular group of people.

Descendant: Someone who is related to a person or group of people who lived in the past.

Deforestation: The act or process of cutting down trees, such as in the rain forest.

Equator: An imaginary circle around the center of the earth.

Indigenous: A word that refers to the very first people to live in an area.

Invertebrate: Without a backbone.

Land Bridge: A connection between two landmasses.

Mammal: A warm-blooded animal that feeds its babies with milk from the mother.

Venomous: Able to cause a poisonous bite or sting.

Kangaroo Quiz Answers

1. True.
2. False. They are herbivores. They eat grasses and leave.
3. True
4. True. The joey usually stays in its mother's pouch for about nine months.
5. False. If they tried, they would probably trip over their tail which can be up to 4 ft. (1.2 m) long.

For Beginning Readers

Available as E-book or Print Edition!

Curious Kids Press

The Elephant Picture Book

With original photography of the elephants at Boon Lott's Elephant Sanctuary in Thailand.

Ages 4-7

By Jack L. Roberts
With Photography by Michael Owens

Other Books from Curious Kids Press

www.curiouskidspress.com

PlanetKids Series (ages 7-9)

PlanetKids: Ancient Egypt

PlanetKids: Australia

PlanetKids: Costa Rica

PlanetKids: France

PlanetKids: Kenya

PlanetKids: Thailand

A Kid's Guide to.. Series (ages 9-12)

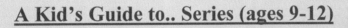

A Kid's Guide to Ancient Egypt

A Kid's Guide to Australia

A Kid's Guide to China

A Kid's Guide to Costa Rica

A Kid's Guide to France

A Kid's Guide to Kenya

A Kid's Guide to Thailand

Other CKP eBooks for Kids

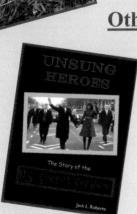

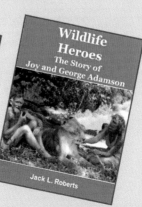

A Kid's Guide to
Australia
For Parents and Teachers

About This Book

A Kid's Guide to . . . is an engaging, easy-to-read book series that provides an exciting adventure into fascinating countries and cultures around the world for young readers. Each book focuses on one country and includes colorful photographs, informational charts and graphs, and quirky and bizarre "Did You Know" facts, all designed to bring the country and its people to life. Designed primarily for recreational, high-interest reading, the informational text series is also a great resource for students to use to research geography topics or writing assignments.

About the Reading Level

A Kid's Guide to . . . is an informational text series designed for kids in grades 4 to 6, ages 9 to 12. For some young readers, the series will provide new reading challenges based on the vocabulary and sentence structure. For other readers, the series will review and reinforce reading skills already achieved. While for still other readers, the book will match their current skill level, regardless of age or grade level.

About the Author

Jack L. Roberts began his career in educational publishing at Children's Television Workshop (now Sesame Workshop), where he was Senior Editor of The Sesame Street/Electric Company Reading Kits. Later, at Scholastic Inc., he was the founding editor of a high-interest/low-reading level magazine for middle school students. Roberts is the author of more than a dozen biographies and other non-fiction titles for young readers, published by Scholastic Inc., the Lerner Publishing Group, Teacher Created Materials, and Benchmark Education. More recently, he was the co-founder of WordTeasers, an educational series of card decks designed to help kids of all ages improve their vocabulary through "conversation, not memorization."